The
Wiersbe
BIBLE STUDY SERIES

The Wiersbe
BIBLE STUDY SERIES

JAMES

Growing

Up in

Christ

DAVID C COOK

transforming lives together

THE WIERSBE BIBLE STUDY SERIES: JAMES
Published by David C Cook
4050 Lee Vance Drive
Colorado Springs, CO 80918 U.S.A.

Integrity Music Limited, a Division of David C Cook
Brighton, East Sussex BN1 2RE, England

The graphic circle C logo is a registered trademark of David C Cook.

All excerpts taken from *Be Mature*, second edition, published by
David C Cook in 2008 © 1978 Warren W. Wiersbe, ISBN 978-1-4347-6845-2.

ISBN 978-0-7814-4571-9
eISBN 978-1-4347-6564-2

The Team: Steve Parolini, Gudmund Lee, Jack Campbell, Theresa With, and Susan Vannaman
Cover Design: John Hamilton Design
Cover Photo: ©iStock

Printed in the United States of America

First Edition 2007

17 18 19 20 21 22 23 24 25 26

062322

Contents

Introduction to James

Beginning a study of a book of the Bible is something like preparing for a trip: You like to know where you are going and what you can expect to see.

Perhaps the best way to launch a study of the epistle of James is to answer three important questions: Who was James? To whom did he write? And why?

Who Was James?

James was a popular name in New Testament times. There were several men who bore this name.

James, the son of Zebedee and brother of John, was one of the most prominent to bear the name. He was a fisherman called by Christ to follow and become a disciple (Matt. 4:18–22). He and his brother John were nicknamed "Sons of Thunder" because of their impulsiveness (Mark 3:17). Killed by Herod in AD 44, James was the first to give his life for Christ (Acts 12:1–2).

James, the son of Alphaeus, was another of the disciples, but little was known about him. There is no indication that this James wrote the letter you are about to study.

There is even less known about James, the father of Judas the disciple (not Judas Iscariot).

James, the half brother of Jesus, seems the most likely candidate for the author of this epistle; however, he does not identify himself in this way. James and the other brothers did not believe in Jesus during His earthly ministry (John 7:1–5; Mark 3:31–35), yet we find them later in the upper room praying with the disciples (Acts 1:14). First Corinthians 15:7 indicates that Jesus appeared to James after His resurrection, which likely was what convinced James that Jesus was truly the Savior.

The James we will discuss became the leader of the church in Jerusalem, and it was he who moderated the church conference described in Acts 15. We have no record in the Bible, but many sources tell us that James was martyred in AD 62.

What kind of man was James? He must have been a deeply spiritual man to gain the leadership of the Jerusalem church in so short a time. Tradition tells us that he was a man of prayer, which explains the emphasis on prayer in his letter.

James was a Jew, reared in the tradition of the law of Moses, and his Jewish legalism stands out in his letter. While still an unbeliever, James must have paid attention to what Jesus taught; numerous allusions to Jesus' sayings, particularly the Sermon on the Mount, appear throughout his letter.

To Whom Did James Write?

James led the church in Jerusalem during a very difficult time, but his letter was directed to the Jews living outside the land of Palestine. James sent his letter to Christian Jews, addressing them as brethren (which indicated they were brothers in Christ Jesus). Christian Jews scattered throughout the Roman Empire had needs and problems unique to their situation. As Jews, they were rejected by Gentiles; and as Christian Jews, they were rejected by their own countrymen.

Why Did James Write?

As you read the epistle, you discover that these Jewish Christians were having some problems in their personal lives and in their church. They were going through difficult trials and facing many temptations. One of the major problems in the church was a failure on the part of many to live what they professed to believe. They also had problems with divisions caused by careless words. And many were dealing with worldliness.

As you review this list of problems, it may look somewhat familiar. Do our churches today not have people who are going through difficult times? Facing trials and temptations? Wrestling with the sins of the tongue and worldliness?

All of the problems James discussed had a common cause: spiritual immaturity. These Christians simply weren't growing up.

The epistle of James logically follows the letter to the Hebrews, for one of the themes of Hebrews is spiritual perfection. The writer of Hebrews explained how perfect salvation could be had in Christ. James' letter exhorts readers to build on this perfect salvation and grow into maturity.

Since the theme of James is spiritual maturity, we must begin by examining our own hearts. This may be a bit uncomfortable at times. There may even be a time in this study when you wonder if continuing is too dangerous. You may want to take an easier way—turn back to your old way of life. Don't do it! When that time arrives, you will be on the verge of a new and wonderful blessing in your own life, a thrilling new step of maturity.

Not everyone who grows old, grows up. There is a difference between age and maturity. Mature Christians are spirit-filled Christians who encourage others and help build their local church.

Welcome to the next step in your spiritual maturity!

—Warren W. Wiersbe

How to Use This Study

This study is designed for both individual and small-group use. We've divided it into eight lessons—each references one or more chapters in Warren W. Wiersbe's commentary *Be Mature*. While reading *Be Mature* is not a prerequisite for going through this study, the additional insights and background Wiersbe offers can greatly enhance your study experience.

The **Getting Started** questions at the beginning of each lesson offer you an opportunity to record your first thoughts and reactions to the study text. This is an important step in the study process as those "first impressions" often include clues about what it is your heart is longing to discover.

The bulk of the study is found in the **Going Deeper** questions. These dive into the Bible text and, along with helpful excerpts from Wiersbe's commentary, help you examine not only the original context and meaning of the verses but also modern application.

Looking Inward narrows the focus down to your personal story. These intimate questions can be a bit uncomfortable at times, but don't shy away from honesty here. This is where you are asked to stand before the mirror of God's Word and look closely at what you see. It's the place to take a good look at yourself in light of the lesson and search for ways in which you can grow in faith.

Going Forward is the place where you can commit to paper those things you want or need to do in order to better live out the discoveries you made in the "Looking Inward" section. Don't skip or skim through this. Take the time to really consider what practical steps you might take to move closer to Christ. Then share your thoughts with a trusted friend who can act as an encourager and accountability partner.

Finally, there is a brief **Seeking Help** section to close the lesson. This is a reminder for you to invite God into your spiritual-growth process. If you choose to write out a prayer in this section, come back to it as you work through the lesson and continue to seek the Holy Spirit's guidance as you discover God's will for your life.

Tips for Small Groups

A small group is a dynamic thing. One week it might seem like a group of close-knit friends. The next it might seem more like a group of uncomfortable strangers. A small-group leader's role is to read these subtle changes and adjust the tone of the discussion accordingly.

Small groups need to be safe places for people to talk openly. It is through shared wrestling with difficult life issues that some of the greatest personal growth is discovered. But in order for the group to feel safe, participants need to know it's okay *not* to share sometimes. Always invite honest disclosure, but never force someone to speak if he or she isn't comfortable doing so. (A savvy leader will follow up later with a group member who isn't comfortable sharing in a group setting to see if a one-on-one discussion is more appropriate.)

Have volunteers take turns reading excerpts from Scripture or from the commentary. The more each person is involved even in the mundane tasks, the more they'll feel comfortable opening up in more meaningful ways.

Finally, soak your group meetings in prayer—before you begin, during as needed, and always at the end of your time together.

Trials
(JAMES 1:1–12)

Before you begin ...
- *Pray for the Holy Spirit to reveal truth and wisdom as you go through this lesson.*
- *Read James 1:1–12. This lesson references chapters 1 and 2 in* Be Mature. *It will be helpful for you to have your Bible and a copy of the commentary available as you work through this lesson.*

Getting Started

From the Commentary

After well over a quarter century of ministry, I am convinced that spiritual immaturity is the number one problem in our churches. God is looking for mature men and women to carry on His work, and sometimes all He can find are little children who cannot even get along with each other.

—*Be Mature,* page 24

1. What is your immediate reaction to these thoughts on spiritual immaturity? Do you agree or disagree? Why? How would you define Christian maturity?

More to Consider: Churches take a variety of approaches to growing spiritual maturity in believers. Some depend on weekly church services and Sunday school classes to provide the meatiest teaching. Others leave the deeper teachings to small groups. Consider your own experience in the church. Where have you found the greatest personal spiritual growth? What does this tell you about today's church—its strengths and weaknesses? What is a good measure of how well a church is growing the maturity of its believers?

2. Choose one verse or phrase from James 1:1–12 that stands out to you. This could be something you're intrigued by, something that makes you uncomfortable, something that puzzles you, something that resonates with you, or just something you want to examine further. Write that here. What strikes you about these verses?

Going Deeper

From the Commentary

> Throughout the Bible are people who turned defeat into victory.... Instead of being victims, they became victors.
>
> James tells us that we can have this same experience today.
>
> —*Be Mature*, page 31

3. Circle the imperatives in James 1:1–12. How do these statements support the idea that Christ-followers can turn defeat into victory? Can you think of examples from Scripture of people who turned defeat into victory? What were the primary reasons they were able to turn that defeat around?

More to Consider: Read John 16:33 and Acts 14:21–25. What do these verses tell us about the inevitability of trials and how we're to respond to them?

From the Commentary

Outlook determines outcome, and attitude determines action. God tells us to *expect trials*. It is not "*if* you fall into various testings" but "*when* you fall into various testings." The believer who expects his Christian life to be easy is in for a shock....

Because we are God's "scattered people" and not God's "sheltered people," we must experience trials. We cannot always expect everything to go our way. Some trials come simply because we are human—sickness, accidents, disappointments, even seeming tragedies. Other trials come because we are Christians.

—*Be Mature*, pages 31–32

4. What words or phrases in James 1:1–12 support this idea that the Christian life is not easy? Underline these. Why does being God's "scattered people" mean that we must experience trials? What sort of "scatteredness" do you think was being experienced by the people to whom James was writing? Which kinds of trials are more difficult to respond to—those that arise because we are humans or those that arise because we are Christians? Explain.

From Today's World

The devastation caused by Hurricane Katrina in 2005 had far-reaching impact. Not only were more than 1,800 people killed and thousands displaced, but also many others lost their jobs, their businesses. The devastation didn't end when the winds died down. Certainly this was (and continues to be for many) a period of great trial.

5. James opens this chapter with a bold challenge to be joyful when facing trials (1:2). How do you think non-Christians who suffered from Katrina would respond to James' challenge? Would this be any different than how Christians might respond? Why do you think this is James' opening statement? In what ways does this statement set the table for what follows?

6. There is a logical progression in James' argument for being joyful about trials: Be joyful because trials produce perseverance and perseverance is how we get to maturity. In other words: Trials bring you to maturity. What does "living for the things that matter most" look like according to James?

From the Commentary

> God builds character before He calls to service. He must
> work *in* us before He can work *through* us. God spent
> twenty-five years working in Abraham before He could
> give him his promised son. God worked thirteen years in
> Joseph's life, putting him into "various testings" before
> He could put him on the throne of Egypt. He spent
> eighty years preparing Moses for forty years of service.
> Our Lord took three years training His disciples, build-
> ing their character.
>
> But God cannot work in us without our consent. There
> must be a surrendered will. The mature person does not
> argue with God's will; instead, he accepts it willingly and
> obeys it joyfully.
>
> —*Be Mature*, page 36

7. James suggests in 1:5 that God will give wisdom to those who ask for it
(and don't doubt God's ability to give that gift). What do you think that
wisdom looks like? How is it given? What relationship is there between this
gift of wisdom and James' earlier comments about trials?

More to Consider: Wiersbe writes, "God wants to make us patient because that's the key to every other blessing." Do you agree or disagree with this statement? Explain.

From the Commentary

When Peter started his walk of faith, he kept his eyes on Christ. But when he was distracted by the wind and waves, he ceased to walk by faith, and he began to sink. He was double-minded, and he almost drowned.

Many Christians live like corks on the waves: up one minute, down the next; tossed back and forth. This kind of experience is evidence of immaturity.

—*Be Mature*, page 39

More to Consider: Read Ephesians 4:7–14. What does Paul say in this passage about the role community plays in growing Christian maturity?

8. How is learning not to doubt God evidence of maturity? In Matthew 14:22–33, what does Peter's experience of walking on water tell you about doubt? About the challenges facing Christians who want to grow in maturity?

9. Reread James 1:9–11. Why do you think James inserts comments about pride and riches in the middle of his treatise on trials? What role does humility play in learning to deal with trials?

From the Commentary

> In James 1:12, James used a very important word: *love*. We would expect him to write, "the crown of life, which the Lord hath promised to them that trust Him" or "that obey Him." Why did James use *love?* Because love is the spiritual motivation behind every imperative in this section.
>
> Why do we have a joyful attitude as we face trials? Because we love God, and He loves us, and He will not harm us.
>
> —*Be Mature*, page 40

10. Verse 12 promises a reward to those who persevere under trial. What is this "crown of life" that James is talking about? How might the promise of this reward be an encouragement for those to whom James writes?

Looking Inward

Take a moment to reflect on all that you've explored thus far in this study of James 1:1–12. Review your notes and answers and think about how each of these things matters in your life today.

Tips for Small Groups: To get the most out of this section, form pairs or trios and have group members take turns answering these questions. Be honest and as open as you can in this discussion, but most of all, be encouraging and supportive of others. Be sensitive to those who are going through particularly difficult times and don't press for people to speak if they're uncomfortable doing so.

11. How are your circumstances like those of the people to whom James writes? What effect does your desire for maturity have on how you deal with the trials you face? How has your humility (or lack thereof) impacted the way you've faced trials?

12. What obstacles (physical, emotional, psychological, relational) make it difficult for you to persevere under trials? How does doubt factor into this?

13. What are some ways you currently seek to become mature in your faith? What new insights did you gain in exploring James 1:1–12 that can help you mature? What does the application of those insights look like in practical terms?

Going Forward

14. Think of one or two things that you have learned that you'd like to work on in the coming week. Remember that this is all about quality, not quantity. It's better to work on one specific area of life and do it well than to work on many and do poorly (or to be so overwhelmed that you simply don't try).

Do you need to work on "hanging in there" in a specific difficult circumstance? Write that here. Do you need to work on humility? On finding joy? On trusting God? What does working on this look like in practical terms? Be specific. Go back through James 1:1–12 and put a star next to the phrase or verse that is most encouraging to you. Consider memorizing this verse so it can encourage you when trials arise.

Real-Life Application Ideas: Choose a trial you're experiencing in life today and talk about it with a trusted friend. Don't shy away from expressing the pain or frustration you're feeling. Ask your friend to help you step back from the circumstance and, together, look for ways God might be using this experience to grow you in maturity. Whether or not you find hints of God's purpose, pray together for wisdom as the circumstance plays out. Then offer to be a listener for any challenging situations your friend may be facing.

Seeking Help

15. Write a prayer below (or simply pray one in silence), inviting God to work on your mind and heart in those areas you noted above. Be honest about your desires and fears.

Notes for Small Groups:

- *Look for ways to put into practice the things you wrote in the "Going Forward" section above. Talk with other group members about your ideas and commit to being accountable to one another.*

- *During the coming week, ask the Holy Spirit to continue to reveal truth to you from what you've read and studied.*

- *Before you start the next lesson, read James 1:13–18. For more in-depth lesson preparation, read chapter 3, "How to Handle Temptation," in* Be Mature.

Temptation
(JAMES 1:13–18)

Before you begin ...
- *Pray for the Holy Spirit to reveal truth and wisdom as you go through this lesson.*
- *Read James 1:13–18. This lesson references chapter 3 in* Be Mature. *It will be helpful for you to have your Bible and a copy of the commentary available as you work through this lesson.*

Getting Started

From the Commentary

The mature person is patient in trials. Sometimes the trials are testings on the outside, and sometimes they are temptations on the inside. Trials may be tests sent by God, or they may be temptations sent by Satan and encouraged by our own fallen nature. It is this second aspect of trials—temptations on the inside—that James dealt with in this section.

We may ask, "Why did James connect the two? What is the relationship between testings without and temptations within?" Simply this: If we are not careful, the testings on the outside may become temptations on the inside.

—*Be Mature*, page 45

1. What is your immediate reaction to these thoughts on the relationship between testings and temptations? Do you agree or disagree? Why?

Both

More to Consider: The story of Job is a vivid illustration of what it feels like to be tested from the outside. Job loses nearly everything he has known, yet he remains steadfast in his love for and trust in God, even after his friends offer a tempting solution to end his suffering: "Curse God and die." What does the manner in which Job's friends attempt to counsel him suggest about the role of discernment in determining where to turn when trials become great? What role should the church play in such circumstances?

The church does nothing helping out being there for widows (see bel.

2. Choose one verse or phrase from James 1:13–18 that stands out to you. This could be something you're intrigued by, something that makes you

Life goes on for all others, while widowers are alone no friends to do thing with together & so on!

uncomfortable, something that puzzles you, something that resonates with you, or just something you want to examine further. Write that here. What strikes you about these verses?

Going Deeper

From the Commentary

> Certainly, God does not want us to yield to temptation, yet neither can He spare us the experience of temptation. We are not God's *sheltered* people; we are God's *scattered* people. If we are to mature, we must face testings and temptations.
>
> —*Be Mature*, page 46

3. Write out the logical progression from temptation to death as described in James 1:13–18. How does temptation mature a Christian's faith?

From the Commentary

> A temptation is an opportunity to accomplish a good thing in a bad way, out of the will of God. Is it wrong to want to pass an examination? Of course not, but if you cheat to pass it, then you have sinned. The temptation to cheat is an opportunity to accomplish a good thing (passing the examination) in a bad way. It is not wrong to eat, but if you consider stealing the food, you are tempting yourself.
>
> —*Be Mature*, page 46

4. What are the primary reasons we are tempted to accomplish good things apart from God? Are all temptations opportunities to accomplish "good" things? Explain.

More to Consider: Read about Eve's temptation in Genesis 3:1–7. What "good thing" was Eve tempted to accomplish? How is this like or unlike the good things we attempt to accomplish today?

From Today's World

It doesn't take much research to find a news story about a well-known Christian leader who has given into temptation. These stories are painful to read because they display the ugly reality of sin on the front page for all to see. But they are, nonetheless, evidence that temptation is no respecter of status or station. Think back on the more recent examples of this sort of public proof of our sinfulness.

5. How does it make you feel to see Christians of such high profiles fail? How does hearing stories like this affect what you think of your ability to stand against temptation? Look at James 1:13–14. How do these verses in particular speak to the universality of temptation?

Christians are so quick to look at a leaders high profile fail, they gossip and say how bad what a shame. Its the same thing about people stuck in a habit or addiction, & christians are quick to also look at the individuals differently, certain Sin they think is bad, well Sin is Sin, Christians seem to catogorize people that sins worse.

From the Commentary

No temptation appears as temptation; it always seems more alluring than it really is. James used two illustrations from the world of sports to prove his point. *Drawn away* carries with it the idea of the baiting of a trap; and *enticed* in the original Greek means "to bait a hook." The hunter and the fisherman have to use bait to attract and catch their prey. No animal is deliberately going to step into a trap and no fish will knowingly bite at a naked hook. The idea is to *hide* the trap and the hook.

TRUE Temptation always carries with it some bait that appeals to our natural desires.

—*Be Mature*, page 47

6. Think about that phrase: "No temptation appears as temptation." If this is true, then how do we determine when we're facing temptation? What clues does James give us about how we can identify it? What natural desires does temptation appeal to?

More to Consider: Wiersbe writes, "Christian living is a matter of the will, not the feelings." How does this statement line up with James' teaching? What role, then, should feelings play in regard to the Christian life?

From the Commentary

> Whenever you are faced with temptation, get your eyes off the bait and look ahead to see the consequences of sin: *the judgment of God.* "For the wages of sin is death" (Rom. 6:23).
>
> —*Be Mature*, page 49

7. How much of a motivation to turn from temptation is the reality of God's judgment? Wiersbe refers to this factor as a negative but important

one. Is fear of judgment a strong enough motivator to fight temptation? Why or why not? *It is diff for all people some of it more than, sin, think about christian Struggle w/ alcohol, drugs, sexual issues, they try, then they fail, then get back up, + or it can take periods or long periods to overcom that habit that is sin, so Are these people not strong enough? Some of the issues are diff to break free & stop*

From the Commentary

> The goodness of God is a great barrier against yielding to temptation. Since God is good, we do not need any other person (including Satan) to meet our needs. It is better to be hungry *in* the will of God than full *outside* the will of God. Once we start to doubt God's goodness, we will be attracted to Satan's offers, and the natural desires within will reach out for his bait.
>
> —*Be Mature*, page 50

8. James makes it abundantly clear that all good comes from God and that this aspect of God's character is unchanging. How can this truth help Christians when faced with temptation? How does using this truth as motivation for turning from temptation compare with the threat of God's judgment?

More to Consider: Read Deuteronomy 6:10–15. In this passage, Moses warns Israel not to forget God's goodness when they enter and enjoy the Promised Land. How is this warning applicable to Christians today?

9. Read James 1:16–18 again. Why does James make such a point to caution believers not to be deceived? What sort of deceptions might believers face concerning the source of temptation? Concerning the source of "all good things"?

From the Commentary

By granting us a new birth, God declares that He cannot accept the old birth. Throughout the Bible, God rejects the firstborn and accepts the secondborn. He accepted Abel, not Cain; Isaac, not Ishmael; Jacob, not Esau. He rejects your first birth (no matter how noble it might have been in the eyes of men), and He announces that you need a second birth.

It is this experience of the new birth that helps us overcome temptation. If we let the old nature (from the first birth) take over, we will fail. We received our old nature (the flesh) from Adam, and he was a failure. But if we yield to the new nature, we will succeed, for that new nature comes from Christ, and He is the Victor.

—*Be Mature*, pages 53–54

10. Verse 18 speaks of being "firstfruits" of God's creation. What are the implications of being God's best and brightest when it comes to temptation? God has given us everything good, including a new nature from Christ. Why then do Christians continue to struggle with temptation? How is learning to rely on the new nature evidence of a growing maturity?

Something I wrote on pg 33 Question 7

Looking Inward

Take a moment to reflect on all that you've explored thus far in this study of James 1:13–18. Review your notes and answers and think about how each of these things matters in your life today.

Tips for Small Groups: To get the most out of this section, form pairs or trios and have group members take turns answering these questions. Be honest and as open as you can in this discussion, but most of all, be encouraging and supportive of others. Be sensitive to those who are going through particularly difficult times and don't press for people to speak if they're uncomfortable doing so.

There needs to be ongoing Support + encouragement even those that struggle w/a sinful habit

11. Have you ever thought of blaming God for your temptations? What prompts this sort of thinking?

12. Consider the many ways temptation entices. What are some of the more compelling lures Satan uses to bait you? In what ways do these lures target your old nature? How would your new nature respond to these lures? How can knowing your weak areas help you better confront temptation?

13. Can you think of examples in your life experience when you recognized a temptation and turned from it? What gave you the strength to turn away? What role did fear of God's judgment play? God's goodness? Your new nature in Christ?

Going Forward

14. Think of one or two things that you have learned that you'd like to work on in the coming week. Remember that this is all about quality, not quantity. It's better to work on one specific area of life and do it well than to work on many and do poorly (or to be so overwhelmed that you simply don't try).

Do you need to work on being more aware of the sorts of lures that Satan uses to tempt you? Write that here. Do you need to discover more about God's goodness? About what it means to be His firstfruits? What does working on this look like in practical terms? Be specific. Go back through James 1:13–18 and put a star next to the phrase or verse that speaks to your greatest area of challenge when it comes to temptation. Consider memorizing this verse so it can help you overcome temptations when they arise.

Real-Life Application Ideas: Pick a day from the preceding week and summarize the events of that day—where you went, what you said, what you did. Then go through that summary and examine it for any choices you made that may have been the result of giving in to temptation. What might you have done differently to avoid or overcome that temptation? Consider these thoughts as you move through the coming days.

Seeking Help

15. Write a prayer below (or simply pray one in silence), inviting God to work on your mind and heart in those areas you noted above. Be honest about your desires and fears.

Notes for Small Groups:
- *Look for ways to put into practice the things you wrote in the "Going Forward" section above. Talk with other group members about your ideas and commit to being accountable to one another.*
- *During the coming week, ask the Holy Spirit to continue to reveal truth to you from what you've read and studied.*
- *Before you start the next lesson, read James 1:19–27. For more in-depth lesson preparation, read chapter 4, "Quit Kidding Yourself," in* Be Mature.

Just Do It
(JAMES 1:19–27)

Before you begin …
- *Pray for the Holy Spirit to reveal truth and wisdom as you go through this lesson.*
- *Read James 1:19–27. This lesson references chapter 4 in* Be Mature. *It will be helpful for you to have your Bible and a copy of the commentary available as you work through this lesson.*

Getting Started

From the Commentary

Many people are deceiving themselves into thinking they are saved when they are not. "Many will say to me in that day, Lord, Lord, have we not prophesied in thy name? and in thy name have cast out devils? and in thy name done many wonderful works? And then will I profess unto them, I never knew you: depart from me, ye that work iniquity" (Matt. 7:22–23).

But there are true believers who are fooling themselves concerning their Christian walk. They think they are spiritual when they are not. It is a mark of maturity when a person faces himself honestly, knows himself, and admits his needs. It is the immature person who pretends, "I am rich, and increased with goods, and have need of nothing" (Rev. 3:17).

—*Be Mature,* page 57

1. What is your initial reaction to these thoughts concerning believers who are fooling themselves about their Christian walk? Do you agree or disagree? Why? The Matthew passage is particularly strong-worded. What overall theme relating to "Christian maturity" do you see when you set this passage next to what James writes in 1:19–27?

More to Consider: James 1:27 brings up a theme that's found not only in the New Testament letters but also in the Gospels—that of "looking after orphans and widows." Who are the orphans and widows in today's society? What are positive examples to illustrate how the church is taking care of orphans and widows? What are some ways the church could improve?

2. Choose one verse or phrase from James 1:19–27 that stands out to you. This could be something you're intrigued by, something that makes you uncomfortable, something that puzzles you, something that resonates with you, or just·something you want to examine further. Write that here. What strikes you about these verses?

Going Deeper

3. Underline all of the words or phrases in James 1:19–27 that relate to speaking or listening. Why do you think James focuses on this theme? What sorts of problems or circumstances might he have been addressing? (Keep in mind he was most likely writing this letter to Christian Jews who had been dispersed and were living outside of Jerusalem.)

Swift to hear, slow to speak, slow to wrath
Doers of the word, not only hearers

From the Commentary

> The final test of salvation is fruit. This means a changed
> life, Christian character and conduct, and ministry to
> others in the glory of God.
>
> —*Be Mature*, page 58

4. The primary focus of James' letter is that a changed life ought to bear
fruit. What does a changed life look like to James? In what ways do
immature Christians deceive themselves about living a changed life? What
is the difference between "manufactured works" and the real fruit of a
relationship with Jesus?

*More to Consider: Read Romans 1:16; 6:22; 15:28; Galatians
5:22–23; Colossians 1:10; and Hebrews 13:15. Each of these passages
describes some sort of fruit that comes from a changed life. Where
do you see these fruits in the lives of Christians? How is each of these
evidence of Christian maturity?*

From the Commentary

✳ We have two ears and one mouth, which ought to remind us to listen more than we speak. Too many times we argue with God's Word, if not audibly, at least in our hearts and minds.

—*Be Mature*, page 59

5. James writes about the importance of being quick to listen and slow to speak. How is this biblical advice ignored or heeded in today's culture? Think of examples from the public arena. Why do you think people tend to reverse these two?

From Today's World

Sins of the tongue make headlines faster than almost any other in today's Internet-driven world. Rumors and truth are spread faster than ever thanks to 24/7 news Web sites and e-mail and blogging. If James were to write this passage today, how do you think he might specifically address how we use these modern methods of communication?

6. James actually gives his readers an opportunity to practice being "quick to listen" in this very passage. Reread James 1:19–27 and spend a moment

reflecting on his words. Did you uncover any new truth this time through? In practical terms, what does it look like to be quick to listen when reading through Scripture?

From the Commentary

> It is not enough to hear the Word; we must do it. Many people have the mistaken idea that hearing a good sermon or Bible study is what makes them grow and get God's blessing. It is not the hearing but *the doing* that brings the blessing. Too many Christians mark their Bibles, but their Bibles never mark them! If you think you are spiritual because you hear the Word, then you are only kidding yourself.
>
> —*Be Mature*, page 61

7. In James 1:22–25, to portray the "immature Christian," James uses the illustration of a man looking into a mirror and forgetting what he looks like after turning away. He contrasts this with the man who looks intently at the "perfect law that gives freedom," offering him up as someone who is growing in maturity. Why do you think he uses the mirror illustration

to describe the immature Christian and yet not when he writes about the mature Christian? In what ways is the "perfect law" a mirror?

More to Consider: James mentions several mistakes people make when they look into God's mirror. Wiersbe describes them this way: They merely glance at themselves; they forget what they see; they fail to obey what the Word tells them to do. How have these mistakes played themselves out in your own experiences?

From the Commentary

After seeing ourselves, we must remember what we are and what God says, and we must *do the Word.* The blessing comes in the doing, not in the reading of the Word.

—*Be Mature,* page 63

8. James says it simply: "Do what [the Word] says." But obviously, this means we have to read the Word first. Is there a difference between simply "reading" the Word and "examining" it? Explain. And if we are to follow

James' admonition to "do," how does that impact the way we're to approach our Bible-reading time?

More to Consider: Read about Nathan's experience with David in 2 Samuel 12. In this passage, Nathan holds up a "mirror" for David to look at himself. What does David see? What is the result of David's glimpse in the mirror?

9. Have you seen examples of the "worthless religion" James writes about in 1:26? Describe them. According to James, how do we know the difference between worthless and acceptable religion?

From the Commentary

> The word translated "religion" means "the outward practice, the service of a god." It is used only five times in the entire New Testament (James 1:26–27; Acts 26:5; and Col. 2:18, where it is translated "worshipping"). Pure religion has nothing to do with ceremonies, temples, or special days. Pure religion means practicing God's Word and sharing it with others, through speech, service, and separation from the world.
>
> *—Be Mature*, page 66

10. James mentions a couple of ways we can practice God's Word (looking after orphans and keeping oneself from being polluted by the world). List other specific ways we can practice God's Word.

Looking Inward

Take a moment to reflect on all that you've explored thus far in this study of James 1:19–27. Review your notes and answers and think about how each of these things matters in your life today.

Tips for Small Groups: To get the most out of this section, form pairs or trios and have group members take turns answering these questions. Be honest and as open as you can in this discussion, but most of all, be encouraging and supportive of others. Be sensitive to those who are going through particularly difficult times and don't press for people to speak if they're uncomfortable doing so.

11. Examine your life and consider specific ways in which you are "doing the Word." What evidence is there that you are living out a changed life?

12. Serving others is one of the more outward signs of an inward change. In what ways are you serving others? What motivates your service?

13. Is it possible to do what the Word says apart from being prompted by a changed life? What is the difference between doing something because

you are compelled to by your heart-change and doing something because you think you're supposed to? How does a growing maturity impact the frequency with which you find yourself living out what James calls "pure religion"?

Going Forward

14. Think of one or two things that you have learned that you'd like to work on in the coming week. Remember that this is all about quality, not quantity. It's better to work on one specific area of life and do it well than to work on many and do poorly (or to be so overwhelmed that you simply don't try).

Do you need to spend more time reading God's Word so you know what it is you're called to do? Do you need to look for specific opportunities to put into practice what you are learning from Scripture? Perhaps you are feeling a specific prompting to live out some truth you've discovered in the Bible. Write these thoughts below. Be specific. Go back through James 1:19–27 and put a star next to the verse that is most convicting to you. Consider memorizing this verse so it can challenge you and move you toward positive change.

Real-Life Application Ideas: Keep a journal of everything you do throughout the day for the next couple of weeks. Do your best to record everything to the smallest detail—who you talk to, what you watch on TV, the errands you run, how you spend money, the tasks you accomplish. After a couple of weeks, tally up the number of things you did for others versus the number of things you did for yourself. Based on these tallies, how well have you been "doing" the Word?

Seeking Help

15. Write a prayer below (or simply pray one in silence), inviting God to work on your mind and heart in those areas you noted above. Be honest about your desires and fears.

Notes for Small Groups:

- *Look for ways to put into practice the things you wrote in the "Going Forward" section above. Talk with other group members about your ideas and commit to being accountable to one another.*

- *During the coming week, ask the Holy Spirit to continue to reveal truth to you from what you've read and studied.*

- *Before you start the next lesson, read James 2:1–26. For more in-depth lesson preparation, read chapters 5 and 6, "Rich Man, Poor Man" and "False Faith," in* Be Mature.

Working Faith
(JAMES 2:1–26)

Before you begin …
- *Pray for the Holy Spirit to reveal truth and wisdom as you go through this lesson.*
- *Read James 2:1–26. This lesson references chapters 5 and 6 in* Be Mature. *It will be helpful for you to have your Bible and a copy of the commentary available as you work through this lesson.*

Getting Started

From the Commentary

Every believer has some statement of faith or personal expression of what he believes. Most churches have such statements and members are asked to subscribe to the statement and practice it. Most churches also have a "covenant" that they read publicly, often when they observe the Lord's Supper. Statements of faith and church covenants are good and useful, but they are not substitutes for doing God's will. As a pastor, I have heard believers read

the church covenant and then come to a business meeting
and act in ways completely contrary to the covenant.

—*Be Mature*, page 71

1. In the previous lesson, we learned the importance of examining the
Word to discover what God desires us to *do* in our expression of a growing
relationship with Him. As you consider Wiersbe's statement above and
James 2:1–26, what are your initial thoughts about what a "working faith"
might look like?

*More to Consider: How well do you know your church's statement of
faith or covenant? Write it here or find out what it says, examine it,
and copy it here. Does it line up with your own beliefs? If not, what
about it is in conflict with your personal theology?*

2. Choose one verse or phrase from James 2:1–26 that stands out to you.
This could be something you're intrigued by, something that makes you
uncomfortable, something that puzzles you, something that resonates

with you, or just something you want to examine further. Write that here. What strikes you about these verses?

Going Deeper

From the Commentary

> *The way we behave toward people indicates what we really believe about God!* We cannot—and dare not—separate *human* relationships from *divine* fellowship.
>
> —*Be Mature,* page 71

3. In what ways does James illustrate the connection between human relationships and divine fellowship? Circle examples of this in James 2:1–26. What does this truth suggest about a person's faith and how it's lived out?

From the Commentary

> The doctrine of God's grace, if we really believe it, forces us to relate to people on the basis of God's plan and not on the basis of human merit or social status. A "class church" is not a church that magnifies the grace of God. When He died, Jesus broke down the wall that separated Jews and Gentiles (Eph. 2:11–22). But in His birth and life, Jesus broke down the walls between rich and poor, young and old, educated and uneducated. It is wrong for us to build those walls again; we cannot rebuild them if we believe in the grace of God.
>
> —*Be Mature*, pages 75–76

4. James' comments about the poor may seem familiar. Take a look at Jesus' Sermon on the Mount in Matthew 5. How do these two passages compare? What specific circumstances do you think James was responding to in this passage? Is anything like this still happening today? Explain.

More to Consider: Read Ephesians 2:11–22. In what ways do Christians continue to build barriers between themselves? Are denominational differences barriers? What about socioeconomic statuses? Lifestyle choices?

How can Christians live out the truth of this passage and remove the walls that separate them?

From the Commentary

> Christian love does not mean that I must *like* a person and agree with him on everything. I may not like his vocabulary or his habits, and I may not want him for an intimate friend. *Christian love means treating others the way God has treated me.* It is an act of the will, not an emotion that I try to manufacture. The motive is to glorify God. The means is the power of the Spirit within ("for the fruit of the Spirit is love"). As I act in love toward another, I may find myself drawn more and more to him, and I may see in him (through Christ) qualities that before were hidden to me.
>
> —*Be Mature,* page 77

5. What is more difficult: loving someone who is different from you or loving someone you just don't like? Jesus would tell us that both kinds of people are our neighbors. James underlines that truth by saying if we don't love our neighbors as ourselves, we're guilty of breaking God's law. In practical terms, describe what it means to love someone you don't like, or someone who is different from you. What would God's love for them look like?

From Today's World

The holocaust may be the most well-known example of what can happen when a group of people are judged by others as inferior, but it is not the only example. Pick up any newspaper or turn on any news channel and you're bound to find a story about ethnic cleansing or genocide happening in Africa and other parts of the world. This is the polar opposite of what James is teaching in 2:1–13.

6. What is your immediate reaction when you read or hear about people's inhumanity to fellow people? What actions, if any, do stories like this prompt in you? How is genocide a form of showing "favoritism"? Does this mean when we judge others in our daily lives that we're no better than those who are leading the charge of ethnic cleansing or other atrocities? Why or why not? Wrestle with this for a bit.

From the Commentary

We shall be judged "by the law of liberty." Why did James use this title for God's law? For one thing, when we obey God's law, it frees us from sin and enables us to walk in liberty (Ps. 119:45). Also, *law prepares us for liberty.* A child must be under rules and regulations because he is not mature enough to handle the decisions and demands of life. He is given *outward discipline* so that he might develop *inward discipline,* and one day be free of rules.

—*Be Mature,* page 79

7. The relationship between law and freedom (or liberty) is a tricky thing to understand. In Matthew 5:17, Jesus says He didn't come to do away with the law, but to fulfill it. How does James speak to this truth in 2:12–13?

From the Commentary

Someone has said that faith is not "believing in spite of evidence, but obeying in spite of consequence." When you read Hebrews 11, you meet men and women who acted on God's Word, no matter what price they had to pay. Faith is not some kind of nebulous feeling that we work up; faith is confidence that God's Word is true and conviction that acting on that Word will bring His blessing.

—*Be Mature,* page 83

8. Underline all the times James states that faith without deeds (or actions) is useless. What does this tell you about James' message? About his understanding of faith? Perhaps you've heard the phrase "Faith is a verb." What does this look like in real life? What is the blessing that comes from acting on your faith?

More to Consider: Read Hebrews 11. Which of these biblical characters do you most relate to? Which inspires you most? In what ways does this list of faithful followers support the truth James presents in 2:14–26?

From the Commentary

Dynamic faith is faith that is real, faith that has power, faith that results in a changed life....

Faith is only as good as its object.... No matter how much faith a person may generate, if it is not directed at the right object, it will accomplish nothing. "I believe" may be the testimony of many sincere people, but the big question is, "In whom do you believe? What do you believe?"

We are not saved by *faith in faith*; we are saved by faith in Christ as revealed in His Word....

True saving faith *leads to action*. Dynamic faith is not intellectual contemplation or emotional consternation; it leads to obedience on the part of the will. And this obedience is not an isolated event: It continues through the whole life. It leads to works.

—*Be Mature,* pages 87–88

9. James uses the example of Abraham and Isaac to demonstrate how faith and actions work together. What other examples from Scripture or your own experience can you think of that illustrate how faith and actions work together? How do these experiences support what Wiersbe says above: "Faith is only as good as its object"?

From the Commentary

James 2 emphasizes that the mature Christian practices the truth. He does not merely hold to ancient doctrines; he practices those doctrines in his everyday life. His faith is not the dead faith of the intellectuals or the demonic faith of the fallen spirits. It is the dynamic faith of men like Abraham and women like Rahab, faith that changes a life and goes to work for God.

—*Be Mature,* page 91

10. What are the ancient doctrines James refers to in chapter 2? What suggestions does James have for how to "practice" the ancient doctrines? Consider your church's statement of faith. In what ways does this (or your own statement of faith) uphold the practice of ancient doctrines in everyday life?

More to Consider: The story of Rahab is particularly powerful because it teaches us that God can use anyone to accomplish his purposes. How does this story tie together the opening part of James 2, where he writes about not showing favoritism, and the second part of James 2, where he writes about what it means to have a living faith?

Looking Inward

Take a moment to reflect on all that you've explored thus far in this study of James 2:1–26. Review your notes and answers and think about how each of these things matters in your life today.

Tips for Small Groups: To get the most out of this section, form pairs or trios and have group members take turns answering the following questions. Be honest and as open as you can in this discussion, but most of all, be encouraging and supportive of others. Be sensitive to those who are going through particularly difficult times and don't press for people to speak if they're uncomfortable doing so.

11. Rewrite James 2:1–12 as if it were directed specifically to you. What sorts of prejudices would James challenge in your life? What would he say about how well you're loving your neighbor as yourself? Which particular "neighbors" might he single out as those to whom you need to show more love?

12. Do a quick self-evaluation of your faith. Is yours more of an intellectual faith or one that is expressed through action? If it's more of an intellectual faith, what would it take to become active?

13. Not all actions of faith are grand and spectacular like Abraham's offering of his son Isaac. What are some of the "smaller" ways you live out a working faith?

Going Forward

14. Think of one or two things you have learned that you'd like to work on in the coming week. Remember that this is all about quality, not quantity. It's better to work on one specific area of life and do it well than to work on many and do poorly (or to be so overwhelmed that you simply don't try).

Do you need to discover new ways to live out your faith? Are there people in your life you need to learn to love more proactively? Perhaps you are feeling a specific prompting to take action on some truth you've discovered while doing this lesson. Write these thoughts below. Be specific. Go back through James 2:1–26 and put a star next to the verse that is most convicting for you. Consider memorizing this verse so it can challenge you and move you toward positive change.

Real-Life Application Ideas: Collect food and clothing and deliver them to a homeless shelter or other organization in order to live out one of James' specific suggestions.

Seeking Help

15. Write a prayer below (or simply pray one in silence), inviting God to work on your mind and heart in those areas you noted above. Be honest about your desires and fears.

Notes for Small Groups:

- *Look for ways to put into practice the things you wrote in the "Going Forward" section above. Talk with other group members about your ideas and commit to being accountable to one another.*

- *During the coming week, ask the Holy Spirit to continue to reveal truth to you from what you've read and studied.*

- *Before you start the next lesson, read James 3:1–12. For more in-depth lesson preparation, read chapter 7, "The World's Smallest but Largest Troublemaker," in* Be Mature.

The Tongue
(JAMES 3:1–12)

Before you begin …
- *Pray for the Holy Spirit to reveal truth and wisdom as you go through this lesson.*
- *Read James 3:1–12. This lesson references chapter 7 in* Be Mature. *It will be helpful for you to have your Bible and a copy of the commentary available as you work through this lesson.*

Getting Started

From the Commentary

The power of speech is one of the greatest powers God has given us. With the tongue, man can praise God, pray, preach the Word, and lead the lost to Christ. What a privilege! But with that same tongue he can tell lies that could ruin a man's reputation or break a person's heart. The ability to speak words is the ability to influence others and accomplish tremendous tasks, and yet we take this ability for granted.

—*Be Mature,* page 98

1. As you read James 3:1–12, what thoughts went through your mind? This particular subject is certainly a universal one—the power of words. Take just a few minutes to think about how you've used words both in uplifting ways and in negative ways. Write your thoughts down here.

More to Consider: Think about the power that our words hold over children. Words can build confidence and maturity in children, or send them spiraling out of control. How have you experienced this truth in your own life, either as a child or as the one speaking words to a child? What can you do to be more conscious of this going forward?

2. Choose one verse or phrase from James 3:1–12 that stands out to you. This could be something you're intrigued by, something that makes you uncomfortable, something that puzzles you, something that resonates with you, or just something you want to examine further. Write that here. What strikes you about these verses?

Going Deeper

From the Commentary

> Apparently, everybody in the assembly wanted to teach and be a spiritual leader, for James had to warn them: "Not many of you should act as teachers, my brothers" (James 3:1 niv). Perhaps they were impressed with the authority and prestige of the office and forgot about the tremendous responsibility *and accountability!* Those who teach the Word face the stricter judgment.
>
> —*Be Mature,* page 98

3. Why do you think James' warning is so stern? In what ways do we hold leaders and teachers in secular society to a higher standard? What sort of responsibilities do teachers of God's Word have that teachers in the secular arena don't? How is this standard determined? What response should Christians have when teachers and leaders don't live up to this standard?

From the Commentary

> The bit and rudder have the power to direct, which means *they affect the lives of others.* A runaway horse or a

shipwreck could mean injury or death to pedestrians or passengers. The words we speak affect the lives of others.

—*Be Mature,* page 100

4. Circle every illustration or metaphor James uses in 3:1–12 to describe the destructive power of the tongue. Then underline all of the examples used to describe the constructive power of the tongue. What do these tell you about James' message? What do these tell you about the specific issues he was likely dealing with that prompted these thoughts?

From the Commentary

A fire can begin with just a small spark, but it can grow to destroy a city. A fire reportedly started in the O'Leary barn in Chicago at 8:30 p.m., October 8, 1871; and because that fire spread, over 100,000 people were left homeless, 17,500 buildings were destroyed, and 300 people died. It cost the city over $400 million.

—*Be Mature,* page 101

5. Think about a recent example of when a spark started a literal or figurative fire. What was the origin of that spark? Was it accidental or intentional? Does the damage caused by something small respect motive? Explain.

More to Consider: The phrase "Loose lips sink ships" gained popularity during World War II because of the literal truth embedded in the words. How is this phrase also true today?

From Today's World

In today's celebrity-obsessed society, rumor has become big business. There are entire publications (and hundreds, if not thousands, of Web sites) dedicated solely to the proliferation of celebrity rumors. Even respected news sources have jumped on the bandwagon, reporting breakups and slipups of the rich and famous as readily as hard-news stories concerning such things as war and the economy.

6. Perhaps you know the phrase "There's no such thing as bad publicity." Do you agree or disagree with this? What might prompt a publicist or agent to claim this sort of idea as truth? What motives drive this kind of thinking? How does this statement line up with James' teaching on the

tongue? Does it prove true in the land of celebrities? How about in smaller circles, like the workplace? Church? Family?

From the Commentary

> One of the sorrows our Lord had to bear when He was here on earth was the way His enemies talked about Him. They called Him a "man gluttonous and a winebibber" (Matt. 11:19) because He graciously accepted invitations to dine with people the Pharisees did not like. When He performed miracles, they said He was in league with Satan. Even when He was dying on the cross, His enemies could not let Him alone but threw vicious taunts into His face.
>
> —*Be Mature*, page 102

7. Children often quote this statement in response to taunts and name-calling: "Sticks and stones can break my bones, but names will never hurt me." As you consider James' teaching in 3:1–12 and Wiersbe's statement above, do you find fault with this statement? Why or why not? How did

Jesus deal with the name-calling? What does this tell us about how we ought to respond? About how we ought to measure our own words?

From the Commentary

Not only is the tongue like a fire, but it is also like a dangerous animal. It is restless and cannot be ruled (unruly), and it seeks its prey and then pounces and kills. My wife and I once drove through a safari park, admiring the animals as they moved about in their natural habitat. But there were warning signs posted all over the park: DO NOT LEAVE YOUR CAR! DO NOT OPEN YOUR WINDOWS! Those "peaceful animals" were capable of doing great damage, and even killing.

Some animals are poisonous, and some tongues spread poison. The deceptive thing about poison is that it works secretly and slowly, and then kills.

—*Be Mature,* page 103

8. Think back on a recent example of how words can damage. This could be something from the public arena or your own life. Now think of a

specific example about the "poisoning" that happens from secrets and rumors. How does the poison of harsh words or rumors spread compared with the retraction of such statements? Why are negative words so much more insidious than positive words?

From the Commentary

> The tongue is also delightful because it is like a tree. In Bible lands, trees are vitally important to the economy: They help to hold down the soil; they provide beauty and shade; and they bear fruit. Our words can help to shelter and encourage a weary traveler, and can help to feed a hungry soul. "The lips of the righteous feed many" (Prov. 10:21). Jesus said, "The words that I speak unto you, they are spirit, and they are life" (John 6:63). As we share His Word with others, we feed them and encourage them along the way.
>
> —*Be Mature,* page 105

9. While James speaks most directly to the destructive power of the tongue, he also alludes to the positive potential of our words by mentioning the tongue's ability to praise. What are some recent examples you've seen or

experienced of the positive power of the tongue? Are these easier or more difficult to recall?

More to Consider: Read Proverbs 10:11; 12:18; and 18:14, 21. How do these verses support James' teaching? Write a few of your own proverbs about the positive power of the tongue.

From the Commentary

The tongue that blesses the Father, and then turns around and curses men made in God's image, is in desperate need of spiritual medicine! How easy it is to sing the hymns during the worship service, then after the service, get into the family car and argue and fight all the way home!

—*Be Mature,* page 106

10. What examples of this two-sided nature of the tongue come to mind as you reflect on the past week at work and home? What sort of "spiritual medicine" helps tame a tongue that curses as well as blesses?

Looking Inward

Take a moment to reflect on all that you've explored thus far in this study of James 3:1–12. Review your notes and answers and think about how each of these things matters in your life today.

> *Tips for Small Groups: To get the most out of this section, form pairs or trios and have group members take turns answering these questions. Be honest and as open as you can in this discussion, but most of all, be encouraging and supportive of others. Be sensitive to those who are going through particularly difficult times and don't press for people to speak if they're uncomfortable doing so.*

11. If you are in a position of leadership, what steps must you take to live up to the standard James refers to in 3:1? How well are you living up to that? If you are considering a leadership or teaching role, how does James' truth impact your thoughts on this?

12. In the past week or two, have you passed along a rumor or otherwise spoken words that could spark a fire? What prompted you to say these things? Would you condone such actions in a church or other spiritual

setting? What can you do to help stop the damage they might cause? If you need to ask for forgiveness from someone, make plans to do that right now.

13. Focus for a moment on the positive, constructive ways you've used your words in recent weeks. How do you feel when you uplift others or praise God with your words? What steps can you take to offer encouraging, healing words instead of destructive ones?

Going Forward

14. Think of one or two things that you have learned that you'd like to work on in the coming week. Remember that this is all about quality, not quantity. It's better to work on one specific area of life and do it well than to work on many and do poorly (or to be so overwhelmed that you simply don't try).

Do you need to work on watching your words better? Does anyone (a family member or close friend) help hold you accountable for the words that come out of your mouth? Do you want to learn how to better praise God? Perhaps you are feeling a specific prompting to live out some truth you've discovered in the Bible. Write these thoughts below. Be specific. Go back through James 3:1–12 and put a star next to the verse that is most convicting to you. Consider memorizing this verse so it can challenge you and move you toward positive change.

Real-Life Application Ideas: Go for a horseback ride and pay close attention to the way the bit directs the horse. Or take a boat ride and observe the power of the tiny rudder. After your ride, spend a few moments in prayer, asking God to direct you, to give you wisdom for all the words you speak.

Seeking Help

15. Write a prayer below (or simply pray one in silence), inviting God to work on your mind and heart in those areas you noted above. Be honest about your desires and fears.

Notes for Small Groups:

- *Look for ways to put into practice the things you wrote in the "Going Forward" section above. Talk with other group members about your ideas and commit to being accountable to one another.*

- *During the coming week, ask the Holy Spirit to continue to reveal truth to you from what you've read and studied.*

- *Before you start the next lesson, read James 3:13–18. For more in-depth lesson preparation, read chapter 8, "Where to Get Wisdom," in* Be Mature.

Wisdom
(JAMES 3:13–18)

Before you begin …
- *Pray for the Holy Spirit to reveal truth and wisdom as you go through this lesson.*
- *Read James 3:13–18. This lesson references chapter 8 in* Be Mature. *It will be helpful for you to have your Bible and a copy of the commentary available as you work through this lesson.*

Getting Started

From the Commentary

Wisdom was an important thing to Jewish people. They realized that it was not enough to have knowledge; you had to have wisdom to be able to use that knowledge correctly. All of us know people who are very intelligent, perhaps almost geniuses, and yet who seemingly are unable to carry out the simplest tasks of life. They can program computers but they cannot manage their own lives! "Wisdom is the principal thing; therefore get wisdom" (Prov. 4:7).

—*Be Mature,* page 111

1. As you read James 3:13–18, what thoughts went through your mind? Is wisdom as important to you as it was to Jewish people? What does society seem to honor more, wisdom or knowledge? Explain.

More to Consider: Wisdom in popular culture is often presented as something rare and difficult to find. In your experience, does wisdom seem distant and unreachable, or something within the grasp of all people? How does this differ from your understanding of "common sense"? How does this line up with what James says in 3:13–18?

2. Choose one verse or phrase from James 3:13–18 that stands out to you. This could be something you're intrigued by, something that makes you uncomfortable, something that puzzles you, something that resonates with you, or just something you want to examine further. Write that here. What strikes you about these verses?

Going Deeper

From the Commentary

> Knowledge enables us to take things apart, but wisdom enables us to put things together and relate God's truth to daily life.
>
> —*Be Mature,* page 111

3. What do you think about Wiersbe's differentiation between knowledge and wisdom? In what ways is this very thought an example of "wisdom that comes from heaven"? The world's definition might be the same as Wiersbe's, except for the words "and relate God's truth to daily life." What do you see as the primary differences between the application of the world's wisdom as compared to heavenly wisdom?

From the Commentary

> The Bible contains many examples of the folly of man's wisdom. The building of the Tower of Babel seemed like a wise enterprise, but it ended in failure and confusion (Gen. 11:1–9). It seemed wise for Abraham to go to Egypt when famine came to Canaan, but the results proved

otherwise (Gen. 12:10–20). King Saul thought it was wise to put his own armor on young David for the lad's battle with Goliath, but God's plan was otherwise (1 Sam. 17:38ff.). The disciples thought it was wise to dismiss the great crowd and let them find their own food; but Jesus took a few loaves and fishes and fed the multitude. The Roman "experts" in Acts 27 thought it was wise to leave port and set sail for Rome, even though Paul disagreed, and the storm that followed proved that Paul's wisdom was better than their expert counsel. They lived to regret it, but they lived!

—*Be Mature*, page 112

4. Underline the characteristics James uses to define heavenly wisdom. Does this look familiar? Some of these same characteristics are used to describe love in 1 Corinthians 13. What role does love play in "heavenly wisdom"?

More to Consider: Look up two or more of the Bible stories mentioned in the above excerpt (Gen. 11:1–9; 12:10–20; 1 Sam. 17:38; and Acts 27; see also Mark 6:30–44). What similarities do you see in how

*the earthly wisdom is offered in each story? What similarities are there
in the heavenly wisdom?*

From the Commentary

> Whenever I ride a bus or elevated train in the city, I
> often think of the man in Boston who was entertaining
> a famous Chinese scholar. He met his Asian friend at the
> train station and rushed him to the subway. As they ran
> through the subway station, the host panted to his guest,
> "If we run and catch this next train, we will save three
> minutes!" To which the patient Chinese philosopher
> replied, "And what significant thing shall we do with the
> three minutes we are saving?"
>
> —*Be Mature,* page 113

5. James 3:14 states that "envy and selfish ambition" are evidence that
certain wisdom is not from heaven. Does either of these apply to the story
Wiersbe tells above? Explain. What are some examples of wisdom born
of envy and selfish ambition? (Keep in mind that both envy and selfish
ambition are inner qualities that can often be hidden under what look like
pure motives.) How do hastiness and patience factor into such motives?

More to Consider: Read Proverbs 9:10. What does the author mean by the "fear of the Lord"? Skim through the rest of Proverbs and underline the descriptions of wisdom that capture your attention.

From Today's World

Scan the "best-sellers" table at any mainstream bookstore and you're bound to find multiple books proclaiming to offer wisdom for one area of life or another (dieting, finances, relational health). Stop by the self-help section of these bookstores and you'll soon discover just how prevalent this sort of book is. Each of these titles promises life-changing solutions, and many are written by experts with advanced degrees.

6. What does the prevalence of self-help books tell you about our world's fascination with "wisdom"? According to James, any wisdom that is not heavenly is "unspiritual" or even "of the devil." How does your experience with these sorts of books line up with James' proclamation? Is James being too harsh on well-meaning wisdom? Explain.

From the Commentary

The origin of true spiritual wisdom is God. To get your wisdom from any other source is to ask for trouble. There is no need to get the counterfeit wisdom of the world, the wisdom that caters to the flesh and accomplishes the work of the Devil. Get your wisdom from God!

—*Be Mature,* page 115

7. How do you get your wisdom from God? List practical ways to increase your heavenly wisdom. (Proverbs will offer lots of clues to this.)

From the Commentary

What a relief it is to turn to the evidences of true spiritual wisdom.

Meekness (James 3:13). Meekness is not weakness; it is power under control....

Purity (v. 17a). "First pure" indicates the importance of holiness. God is holy; therefore the wisdom from above is pure....

Peace (v. 17b). Man's wisdom leads to competition, rivalry, and war (James 4:1–2); but God's wisdom leads to peace. It is a peace based on holiness, not on compromise....

Gentleness (v. 17c). [English poet and critic] Matthew Arnold liked to call this "sweet reasonableness." It carries the meaning of moderation without compromise, gentleness without weakness....

Compliance (v. 17d). *God's* wisdom makes the believer agreeable and easy to live with and work with....

Mercy (v. 17e). To be "full" of something means to be "controlled by" [it]. The person who follows God's wisdom is controlled by mercy....

Good fruits (v. 17f). People who are faithful are fruitful....

Decisiveness (v. 17g). The word suggests singleness of mind and is the opposite of "wavering" (James 1:6)....

Sincerity (v. 17h). The Greek word translated "hypocrite" in our New Testament means "one who wears a mask, an actor." When man's wisdom is at work, there may be insincerity and pretense. When God's wisdom is at work, there is openness and honesty, "speaking the truth in love" (Eph. 4:15).

—*Be Mature,* pages 117–19

8. Review the traits listed above. How have you seen these in action in your church life? In your small group? If true wisdom comes from humility and not grandstanding or clever advertising, what then draws people to those who are wise?

From the Commentary

Origin determines outcome. Worldly wisdom will produce worldly results; spiritual wisdom will give spiritual results.

Worldly wisdom produces trouble (3:16): envy, strife, confusion, evil works. It does not appear that God was at work in that assembly. In James 4, James would deal with the "wars and fightings" among the believers. Wrong thinking produces wrong living. One reason the world is in such a mess is because men have refused to accept the wisdom of God.

—*Be Mature,* page 120

9. Describe some ways the world is in such a mess because men have "refused to accept the wisdom of God." Now look at each of those circumstances and consider how things might be different if men had accepted God's wisdom. What influence can Christians have on turning those circumstances around? How do we do that?

More to Consider: Read 2 Corinthians 12:20. This is a description of a church that is clearly in disorder. What sort of "worldly wisdom" could have caused this disorder? How is this church like or unlike your own?

From the Commentary

> What we are is what we live, and what we live is what we sow. What we sow determines what we reap. If we live in God's wisdom, we sow righteousness and peace, and we reap God's blessing. If we live in man's worldly wisdom, we sow sin and war, and we reap "confusion and every evil work."
>
> —*Be Mature*, page 121

10. In the above excerpt, Wiersbe restates the thread that runs through all of James—by its very nature, a life of faith will sow things that are good. What are some of the things Christians ought to be sowing into the world? How are we doing with that? How can we sow righteousness and peace more effectively?

Looking Inward

Take a moment to reflect on all that you've explored thus far in this study of James 3:13–18. Review your notes and answers and think about how each of these things matters in your life today.

Tips for Small Groups: To get the most out of this section, form pairs or trios and have group members take turns answering these questions. Be honest and as open as you can in this discussion, but most of all, be encouraging and supportive of others. Be sensitive to those who are going through particularly difficult times and don't press for people to speak if they're uncomfortable doing so.

11. Would you consider yourself wise? Why or why not? What deeds or actions would suggest you're living out heavenly wisdom? What deeds or actions suggest you're counting on worldly wisdom?

12. Review the traits listed above question 8 again. Which of these are evident in your life? Which are notably absent?

13. Take a close look at those places in your life where you tend to be selfish or envious. What prompts those feelings or actions? What would those areas of life look like if you sought heavenly wisdom instead? How do you go about doing that?

Going Forward

14. Think of one or two things that you have learned that you'd like to work on in the coming week. Remember that this is all about quality, not quantity. It's better to work on one specific area of life and do it well than to work on many and do poorly (or to be so overwhelmed that you simply don't try).

Do you need to study Scripture more to gain a better understanding of wisdom? Do you need to learn humility? Do you feel led to speak godly wisdom into a circumstance where worldly wisdom currently rules? How will you do that? Perhaps you are feeling a specific prompting to live out some truth you've discovered in the Bible. Write these thoughts below. Be specific. Go back through James 3:13–18 and put a star next to the verse that is most convicting to you. Consider memorizing this verse so it can challenge you and move you toward positive change.

Real-Life Application Ideas: Go to your local bookstore and skim through a number of books that proclaim to offer wisdom. Compare what you read to what James says about heavenly wisdom. In what ways do these books agree with or disagree with James' definition of wisdom?

Seeking Help

15. Write a prayer below (or simply pray one in silence), inviting God to work on your mind and heart in those areas you noted above. Be honest about your desires and fears.

Notes for Small Groups:

- *Look for ways to put into practice the things you wrote in the "Going Forward" section above. Talk with other group members about your ideas and commit to being accountable to one another.*

- *During the coming week, ask the Holy Spirit to continue to reveal truth to you from what you've read and studied.*

- *Before you start the next lesson, read James 4:1–17. For more in-depth lesson preparation, read chapters 9 and 10, "How to End Wars" and "Plan Ahead," in* Be Mature.

God's Will
(JAMES 4:1–17)

Before you begin …
- *Pray for the Holy Spirit to reveal truth and wisdom as you go through this lesson.*
- *Read James 4:1–17. This lesson references chapters 9 and 10 in* Be Mature. *It will be helpful for you to have your Bible and a copy of the commentary available as you work through this lesson.*

Getting Started

From the Commentary

James began chapter 4 talking about war with God, and he ended it talking about the will of God. But the two themes are related: When a believer is out of the will of God, he becomes a troublemaker and not a peacemaker.

—*Be Mature,* page 137

1. As you read James 4:1–17, what thoughts went through your mind? What does it mean to be in "the will of God"? How does being in God's will impact the way we are to relate to others?

2. Choose one verse or phrase from James 4:1–17 that stands out to you. This could be something you're intrigued by, something that makes you uncomfortable, something that puzzles you, something that resonates with you, or just something you want to examine further. Write that here. What strikes you about these verses?

Going Deeper

From the Commentary

When you examine some of the early churches, you discover that they had their share of disagreements. The members of the Corinthian church were competing with

each other in the public meetings, and even suing each
other in court (1 Cor. 6:1–8; 14:23–40). The Galatian
believers were "biting and devouring" one another (Gal.
5:15). Paul had to admonish the Ephesians to cultivate
spiritual unity (Eph. 4:1–16), and even his beloved church
at Philippi had problems: Two women could not get along
with each other (Phil. 4:1–3).

—*Be Mature,* page 126

3. Unity among believers is a common theme in Paul's letters to the early
church. How does James speak to this same issue in 4:1–3? What sorts of
"wrong motives" can lead to fights and quarrels?

From the Commentary

The essence of sin is selfishness. Eve disobeyed God
because she wanted to eat of the tree and become wise
like God. Abraham lied about his wife because he selfishly wanted to save his own life (Gen. 12:10–20). Achan
caused defeat to Israel because he selfishly took some
forbidden loot from the ruins of Jericho (Josh. 7). "We
have turned every one to his own way" (Isa. 53:6).

—*Be Mature,* page 128

4. James states that "friendship with the world is hatred toward God." Is friendship with the world the same thing as sin? Explain. How is "selfishness" an example of friendship with the world?

More to Consider: Read about Abraham's lie in Genesis 12:10–20. What prompted the "father of a nation" to lie? What does this story tell you about the pervasive nature of selfishness?

From the Commentary

> The root cause of every war, internal and external, is rebellion against God. At the beginning of creation, you behold perfect harmony, but sin came into the world, and this led to conflict. Sin is lawlessness (1 John 3:4), and lawlessness is rebellion against God.
>
> —*Be Mature,* page 129

5. Recall the fights or arguments you've observed or experienced recently. What was the catalyst for these battles? In what ways were they examples of rebellion toward God?

More to Consider: James compares friendship with the world to adultery because believers are considered "married to Christ." Hosea uses the same sort of imagery (Hosea 1—2). How does this picture of a broken relationship with God impact the way you perceive sin and lawlessness?

From the History Books

World War I began essentially because of the death of Archduke Franz Ferdinand, the heir to the Austro-Hungarian throne. When Austria-Hungary determined Serbia hadn't punished those responsible for Ferdinand's death, they declared war. It was only a matter of weeks before major European powers had joined the war, thanks to international alliances and agreements. The archduke's assassination set into motion events that eventually let to the Great War.

6. James writes about the dangerous nature of pride and judgment. As you consider WWI (or any war for that matter), what role might pride or judgment of others have played in the genesis of this war? What role do pride and judgment play in the continuation of war? James tells his readers to humble themselves and submit to God and that will lead to joy. How could humility have helped to prevent WWI? How is seeking humility an example of pursuing God's will?

From the Commentary

> God graciously draws near to us when we deal with the
> sin in our lives that keeps Him at a distance. He will not
> share us with anyone else; He must have complete control.
> The double-minded Christian can never be close to God.
> Again, Abraham and Lot come to mind. Abraham "drew
> near" and talked to God about Sodom (Gen. 18:23ff.),
> while Lot moved into Sodom and lost the blessing of God.
>
> —*Be Mature,* page 133

7. What does it mean to be "double-minded"? How does the pursuit of
God's will help keep Christians from double-mindedness? James tells his
readers that when they resist the Devil, he will flee from them. How does
someone go about doing this? Describe what it looks like in practical terms
to come near to God.

From the Commentary

> Apart from the will of God, life is a mystery. When you
> know Jesus Christ as your Savior and seek to do His will,

then life starts to make sense. Even the physical world around you takes on new meaning. There is a simplicity and unity to your life that makes for poise and confidence. You are no longer living in a mysterious, threatening universe. You can sing, "This is my Father's world!"

—*Be Mature,* pages 138–39

8. In 4:13–17, James is addressing people who seem to "have it all together" in life, those who have everything in order and are confident in their plans for the future. Perhaps you know people like this today. How might these people respond to James' challenge to their "boasting about tomorrow"? What is James' answer to the uncertainty of tomorrow?

From the Commentary

Everything in this universe operates according to laws. If we cooperate with these laws and obey them, then the universe works *with* us. But if we fight these laws and disobey them, the universe will work *against* us. For example, certain laws govern flight. The engineer who obeys those laws in designing and building the plane and the pilot who obeys those laws in flying the plane will both have the joy of seeing the great machine operate perfectly. But if they disobey the basic laws that govern flight, the result will be a crash and the loss of life and money.

God's will for our lives is comparable to the laws He has built within the universe, with this exception: Those laws are general, but the will He has planned for our lives is specifically designed for us. No two lives are planned according to the same pattern.

—*Be Mature,* pages 142–43

9. List some of the "general laws" God has built into the universe, then consider what would happen if people disobeyed those laws. Think about Christians you know and the paths their lives have taken. What are some of the unique ways people are living out God's will?

From the Commentary

The secret of a happy life is to delight in duty. When duty becomes delight, then burdens become blessings. "Thy statutes have been my songs in the house of my pilgrimage" (Ps. 119:54). When we love God, then His statutes become songs, and we enjoy serving Him. When we serve God grudgingly, or because we have to, we may accomplish His work but we ourselves will miss the blessing. It will be toil, not ministry. But when we do God's will from the heart, we are enriched, no matter how difficult the task might have been.

—*Be Mature,* page 145

10. James' admonition to humble ourselves before God is also an invitation to delight in duty, as Wiersbe writes. What are the greatest challenges to adopting this sort of attitude? Does serving God begrudgingly still grow a believer's maturity? Why or why not? What are some practical ways to measure whether we're serving God out of love or because we feel we have to? How does someone move from begrudging service to willing service?

Looking Inward

Take a moment to reflect on all that you've explored thus far in this study of James 4:1–17. Review your notes and answers and think about how each of these things matters in your life today.

Tips for Small Groups: To get the most out of this section, form pairs or trios and have group members take turns answering these questions. Be honest and as open as you can in this discussion, but most of all, be encouraging and supportive of others. Be sensitive to those who are going through particularly difficult times and don't press for people to speak if they're uncomfortable doing so.

11. In what ways does your pride cause fights or quarrels with family members, coworkers, or friends? What is at the root of that pride? How different would those relationships be if you took on an attitude of humility? How do you go about doing that?

12. Think of a time when you sat in judgment of others. What prompted your judgmental attitude? If you were pursuing God's will in that circumstance, how might your attitude have been different?

13. When you read James' pronouncement that we are like "mist," how does that make you feel? How does it impact the manner in which you live your life? How should it? What changes need to occur in your life in order for you to pursue the Lord's will in everything? How does the concept of "planning" take on new significance in light of pursuing God's will?

Going Forward

14. Think of one or two things that you have learned that you'd like to work on in the coming week. Remember that this is all about quality, not quantity. It's better to work on one specific area of life and do it well than to work on many and do poorly (or to be so overwhelmed that you simply don't try).

Do you need to ask forgiveness from someone you have wronged? Do you need to work on personal issues with pride or a judgmental attitude?

Perhaps you are feeling a specific prompting to live out some truth you've discovered in the Bible. Write those thoughts below. Be specific. Go back through James 4:1–17 and put a star next to the verse that is most convicting to you. Consider memorizing this verse so it can challenge you and move you toward positive change.

Real-Life Application Ideas: Interview one or more mature Christians on the subject of God's will. Ask how they've gone about seeking God's will and what obstacles they've faced as they've tried to interpret the right path to walk. If you have specific questions about your own spiritual journey, talk about these together. Spend time in prayer seeking wisdom for your next steps.

Seeking Help

15. Write a prayer below (or simply pray one in silence), inviting God to work on your mind and heart in those areas you noted above. Be honest about your desires and fears.

Notes for Small Groups:

- *Look for ways to put into practice the things you wrote in the "Going Forward" section above. Talk with other group members about your ideas and commit to being accountable to one another.*

- *During the coming week, ask the Holy Spirit to continue to reveal truth to you from what you've read and studied.*

- *Before you start the next lesson, read James 5:1–20. For more in-depth lesson preparation, read chapters 11, 12, and 13, "Money Talks," "The Power of Patience," and "Let us Pray," in* Be Mature.

Patience
(JAMES 5:1–20)

Before you begin ...
- *Pray for the Holy Spirit to reveal truth and wisdom as you go through this lesson.*
- *Read James 5:1–20. This lesson references chapters 11, 12, and 13 in* Be Mature. *It will be helpful for you to have your Bible and a copy of the commentary available as you work through this lesson.*

Getting Started

From the Commentary

James was still addressing the suffering saints when he wrote, "Be patient." This was his counsel at the beginning of his letter (James 1:1–5) and his counsel as his letter came to a close. God is not going to right all the wrongs in this world until Jesus Christ returns, and we believers must patiently endure—and expect.

Three times James reminded us of the coming of the Lord

(James 5:7–9). This is the "blessed hope" of the Christian (Titus 2:13). We do not expect to have everything easy and comfortable in this present life.

—*Be Mature,* page 161

1. What is the first thing that comes to mind when you hear the word patience? Do you find it easy or difficult to be patient in life? For what kinds of things are you least patient? What role has patience played in your faith journey thus far?

2. Choose one verse or phrase from James 5:1–20 that stands out to you. This could be something you're intrigued by, something that makes you uncomfortable, something that puzzles you, something that resonates with you, or just something you want to examine further. Write that here. What strikes you about these verses?

Going Deeper

From the Commentary

The Bible does not discourage the acquiring of wealth. In the law of Moses, specific rules are laid down for getting and securing wealth. The Jews in Canaan owned their own property, worked it, and benefited from the produce. In several of His parables, Jesus indicated His respect for personal property and private gain. There is nothing in the Epistles that contradicts the right of private ownership and profit.

What the Bible does condemn is acquiring wealth by illegal means or for illegal purposes.... What we possess and use are merely things, apart from the will of God. When we yield to His will and use what He gives us to serve Him, then things become treasures and we are investing in eternity.

—*Be Mature,* pages 150, 153

3. Before he speaks specifically about patience, James offers a stern warning to rich oppressors. What significance, if any, do you see in James' decision to address this subject just before encouraging readers to be patient in the face of suffering? What sort of circumstances might have prompted James to speak so harshly to those who have lived in "self-indulgence"?

From the Commentary

> It is good to have the things that money can buy, pro-
> vided you also have the things that money cannot buy.
> What good is a $500,000 house if there is no home? Or
> a million-dollar diamond ring if there is no love? James
> did not condemn riches or rich people; he condemned the
> wrong use of riches, and rich people who use their wealth
> as a weapon and not as a tool with which to build.
>
> —*Be Mature,* page 157

4. Look up Matthew 19:16–24. How is James' rebuke of the wrong use of riches like the message of Jesus' parable? James seems to be saying that there are no "shortcuts" to blessings. In what ways do people attempt to shortcut their way to riches and success? Do people attempt this with their spiritual growth, too? Explain.

More to Consider: Wiersbe writes, "There is a great difference between enjoying what God has given us (1 Tim. 6:17) and living extravagantly on what we have withheld from others." What is the great difference he is referring to? How might James answer that question?

From the Commentary

> Here, then, is a secret of endurance when the going is tough: *God is producing a harvest in our lives.* He wants the "fruit of the Spirit" to grow (Gal. 5:22–23), and the only way He can do it is through trials and troubles. Instead of growing impatient with God and with ourselves, we must yield to the Lord and permit the fruit to grow. We are "spiritual farmers" looking for a harvest.
>
> —*Be Mature*, page 163

5. The New Testament uses the theme of "sowing and reaping" often because it would have been culturally relevant to the people. What illustrations from modern culture might offer similar lessons? What are some examples of what it means to persevere when times are tough? How do perseverance and patience work together in God's economy?

More to Consider: In John 16:33, Jesus says that we'll have trouble in this life, but also to "take heart" because He has overcome the world. What are examples of "trouble" you've seen in the world around you?

From Today's World

The proliferation of "get rich quick" schemes offered on late-night television and in your local bookstore is a testament to our culture's hunger for wealth and prosperity, and disdain for patience. Many of these programs promise some "secret" solution that only a few people have access to (but you, too, can be one of the few if you just sign up today … and pay a lot of money). Perhaps you've even tried one of these programs (or perhaps just skimmed through a book or two).

6. In what ways are these "get rich quick" schemes evidence of a deeper need in American culture? Are there any aspects of our American culture where patience is held up as a virtue? What does this tell us about our priorities? What would James say our priority ought to be in this life? How can we, as members of Jesus' church, help society move toward that way of life?

From the Commentary

> "As you know, we consider blessed those who have persevered" (James 5:11 niv). But you cannot persevere unless there is a trial in your life. There can be no victories without battles; there can be no peaks without valleys. If you want the blessing, you must be prepared to carry the burden and fight the battle.
>
> —*Be Mature,* page 165

7. James singles out Job as a man who persevered through trials. Skim through the book of Job and underline some of the trials he endured (see Job 1—2). Then circle the blessings he received on the other side of his season of tribulation (see Job 42). Job's blessings were certainly measurable, but is this always the case? What other examples of blessing have you observed in the lives of those who have suffered?

From the Commentary

> One of the purposes of suffering is the building of character. Certainly Job was a better man for having gone

through the furnace. (James explained this process to us, James 1:2–12.) If words are a test of character, then oaths would indicate that there is yet work to be done. When Peter poured out those oaths in the courtyard (Matt. 26:71), he was giving evidence that his character was still in need of a transformation.

—*Be Mature,* page 169

8. What are some godly character traits that come from suffering? Are these traits that could come in any other ways? Explain. If even Peter was in need of transformation (as Wiersbe states), then what does that say about the rest of us?

From the Commentary

Prayer can remove affliction, if that is God's will. But prayer can also give us the grace we need to endure troubles and use them to accomplish God's perfect will. *God can transform troubles into triumphs.* "He giveth more grace" (James 4:6). Paul prayed that God might change his circumstances, but instead, God gave Paul the grace he needed to turn his weakness into strength (2 Cor. 12:7–10). Our Lord prayed in Gethsemane that the cup might be removed, and it was not, yet the Father gave Him the strength He needed to go to the cross and die for our sins.

—*Be Mature*, page 174

9. Prayer may seem a great mystery, especially when it comes to helping those who suffer from affliction, but James puts it rather plainly: Just do it. What is your initial reaction to this proclamation? Does this suggest that a "greater faith" results in a greater likelihood of answered prayer? Why or why not? In what ways do Wiersbe's observations shed light on James' words?

From the Commentary

Prayer power is the greatest power in the world today. "Tremendous power is made available through a good man's earnest prayer" (James 5:16 ph). History shows how mankind has progressed from manpower to horsepower, and then to dynamite and TNT, and now to nuclear power.

But greater than nuclear power is prayer power. Elijah prayed for his nation, and God answered prayer. We need to pray for our nation today, that God will bring conviction and revival, and that "showers of blessing" will come to the land.

—*Be Mature,* page 179

10. What significance, if any, is there to James' decision to weave his thoughts about prayer among his thoughts on confession and forgiveness? James refers to Elijah as a man who, though "just like us," prayed earnestly and saw answers to those prayers. Why do you think James made the point to state that Elijah was "just like us"?

Looking Inward

Take a moment to reflect on all that you've explored thus far in this study of James 5:1–20. Review your notes and answers and think about how each of these things matters in your life today.

Tips for Small Groups: To get the most out of this section, form pairs or trios and have group members take turns answering these questions. Be honest and as open as you can in this discussion, but most of all, be encouraging and supportive of others. Be sensitive to those who are going through particularly difficult times and don't press for people to speak if they're uncomfortable doing so.

11. Take a look at your own heart as it relates to money and wealth. What might James want to say to you if he could see what you see?

12. According to James, patience is not only a virtue, it's also the path to blessing and spiritual maturity. How patient are you? In what areas of life are you least patient? Do you see trials as opportunities for growth? Why or why not? If you look back on the challenges you've faced in the past year, can you see ways in which God has been growing you? Explain.

13. How does your prayer life line up with James' teaching on prayer? What does it look like to offer prayer in faith? What role does faith play in your expectations for answers to prayer?

Going Forward

14. Think of one or two things that you have learned that you'd like to work on in the coming week. Remember that this is all about quality, not quantity. It's better to work on one specific area of life and do it well than to work on many and do poorly (or to be so overwhelmed that you simply don't try).

Do you need to reevaluate your priorities when it comes to money? Do you need to work on persevering through a specific trial? Do you need to develop a more faithful prayer life? Perhaps you are feeling a specific prompting to live out some truth you've discovered in the Bible. Write these thoughts below. Be specific. Go back through James 5:1–20 and put a star next to the verse that is most convicting to you. Consider memorizing this verse so it can challenge you and move you toward positive change.

Real-Life Application Ideas: Choose a night to get together with your closest friends for a time of prayer and shared suffering. Invite each person to share a difficult circumstance they're going through and then take the time to pray together, asking God not only to provide an answer to the difficult circumstance, but also to grow the sufferer's spiritual maturity through the trials or valleys. Consider meeting regularly to support one another through difficult times.

Seeking Help

15. Write a prayer below (or simply pray one in silence), inviting God to work on your mind and heart in those areas you noted above. Be honest about your desires and fears.

Notes for Small Groups:

- *Look for ways to put into practice the things you wrote in the "Going Forward" section above. Talk with other group members about your ideas and commit to being accountable to one another.*
- *During the coming week, ask the Holy Spirit to continue to reveal truth to you from what you've read and studied.*

Summary and Review

Notes for Small Groups: This session is a summary and review of this book. Because of that, it is shorter than the previous lessons. If you are using this in a small-group setting, consider combining this lesson with a time of fellowship or a shared meal.

> *Before you begin …*
> - *Pray for the Holy Spirit to reveal truth and wisdom as you go through this lesson.*
> - *Briefly review the notes you made in the previous sessions. You'll be referring to previous chapters throughout this bonus lesson.*

Looking Back

1. Over the past eight lessons, you've been examining what it means to grow in maturity. Now that you've spent lots of time with James' words,

how would you define Christian maturity? Has your definition changed at all from when you first started this study? Why or why not?

2. What is the most significant personal discovery you've made from this study of James?

3. What surprised you most about the book of James? What, if anything, troubled you?

Progress Report

4. Take a few moments to review the "Going Forward" sections of the previous lessons. How would you rate your progress for each of the things you chose to work on? What adjustments, if any, do you need to make to continue on the path toward spiritual maturity?

5. In what ways have you grown closer to Christ during this study? Take a moment to celebrate those things. Then think of areas where you feel you still need to grow and note those here. Make plans to revisit this study in a few weeks to review your growing faith.

Things to Pray About

6. James packs a lot of challenges in his letter. You may feel overwhelmed at times when considering all that he writes about. Take a few minutes to pray

for a greater understanding of God's truth and that God would reveal to you just what He wants you to discover among all the wisdom and admonition.

7. Taking a step or two toward maturity is a great thing. But like so much of life, you may sometimes feel like you're taking two steps back for every step forward. Take a few minutes to ask God to help cement the learning in your heart so it becomes your new nature.

8. Whether you've been studying this in a small group or on your own, there are many other Christians working through the very same issues you discovered when exploring James. Take time to pray for each of them, that God would reveal truth, that the Holy Spirit would guide you, and that each person might grow in spiritual maturity according to God's will.

A Blessing of Encouragement

Studying the Bible is one of the best ways to learn how to be more like Christ. Thanks for taking this step. In closing, let this blessing precede you and follow you into the next week while you continue to marinate in God's Word:

May God light your path to greater understanding as you review the truths found in the book of James and consider how they can help you grow closer to Christ.